WOW! Wildlife

Amazing Animal Homes

by Alix Wood

WINDMILL BOOKS

New York

Published in 2013 by Windmill Books,
An Imprint of Rosen Publishing
29 East 21st Street, New York, NY 10010

Editor for Alix Wood Books: Mark Sachner
US Editor: Sara Antill
Designer: Alix Wood
Consultant: Sally Morgan

Photo Credits: Cover, 1, 2, 3, 4, 5, 6, 7, 8, 9 (top), 10, 11, 12, 13 (top & middle), 14, 15 (bottom), 16, 17 (bottom),
18, 19 (top), 20, 21, 22, 23 © Shutterstock; 9 (bottom) © PHGCOM; 13 (bottom) © Michael Geary;
15 (top) © istock; 17 (top) © Manuel Mejia; 19 (bottom) © Getty Images

Library of Congress Cataloging-in-Publication Data

Wood, Alix.
  Amazing animal homes / by Alix Wood.
      p. cm. — (Wow! wildlife)
  Includes index.
  ISBN 978-1-4488-8098-0 (library binding) — ISBN 978-1-4488-8162-8 (pbk.) —
ISBN 978-1-4488-8169-7 (6-pack)
  1. Animals—Habitations—Juvenile literature. I. Title.
  QL756.W58 2013
  591.56'4—dc23

                              2012005293

Manufactured in the United States of America

CPSIA Compliance Information: Batch #B1S12WM: For Further Information contact Windmill Books, New York, New York at 1-866-478-0556

Contents

What Is a Home?

Many animals need homes, just as people do. Homes provide shelter and a safe place to sleep. They also give animals a place to look after their young.

Animals live in many different kinds of homes, like this baby albatross in its nest. They make homes that are perfect for them, even if they seem a little strange to us!

Some animals live in big groups called **colonies**. Many bat colonies spend the winter sleeping in caves where it is dry and safe.

WOW! Underground Crab City

Lots of animals choose to live underground in **burrows**. These fiddler crabs' beach burrows give safety from the Sun and from predators. When high tide covers their homes, fiddler crabs plug the chimney holes with balls of mud, trapping air inside the burrows. The crabs can breathe the trapped air until the tide goes out and uncovers the burrows again!

Giant Homes for Tiny Insects

Termites build amazing mounds that are home to several million insects. Made with soil, mud, chewed wood, spit, and **dung**, these mounds can be as tall as a three-story building!

African termites build the largest **structures** in the animal world. The material they build with is so hard and waterproof that local people use it for concrete and cement!

Life-size termites

6

WOW! The Ant Dome

What looks like a messy heap of leaves and twigs is actually a nest made by wood ants (right). Sometimes many nests make up super colonies. Don't get too close! Worker ants squirt **formic acid** if disturbed.

In hot areas, compass termites build tall, wedge-shaped mounds. These act like cooling chimneys for the nests below. The broad sides face the weaker morning and evening Sun. The thin end of the nest faces toward the Sun at its hottest. Less surface heating up at hot times of the day helps the termites stay cool!

The temperature in a termite mound is so even that monitor lizards break in and lay their eggs in them. It is the perfect temperature for the eggs to hatch!

7

Insect Master Builders

Bees and wasps live in big communities. They work together to build their nests and feed and care for their young. The nests are made up of lots of tiny cells. The insects lay their eggs in the cells. Bees store food in the cells, too.

Honeybees make their nests out of wax. The wax is made in a **gland** in the worker bee's body. The bees use their legs to shape this wax into lots of **hexagonal** cells. This is called honeycomb. The honeycomb cells hold honey, or a baby bee. In winter, honeybees feed on the honey they made in the summer.

Young **larvae** are looked after by adult honeybees in their cells. The workers protect the young and the egg-laying queen.

Some wasps make their nests out of paper. They chew up wood and mix it with spit. The queen starts building the nest. She catches an insect to put in each cell. She then lays an egg in the same cell. When the egg hatches, the **larva** eats the insect. When enough female workers are born, they take over building the nest. Some wasp nests can be as big as a beach ball!

A queen starting to build the nest

WOW! Weaver Ants Teamwork

Weaver ants work together to build a nest out of leaves held together by silk made by their larvae! A few ants bend a leaf over. Other workers then help join the leaf to another leaf. If the gap between two leaves is too big to pull them together, the ants make a chain by holding each other's waists. Then they get some larvae and hold them on the joint until the larvae produce silk. This sticks the leaves together!

Safety Up High

Many animals look for safety up high, away from danger, to make their homes.

Bats hunt during the night and sleep in the daytime. They sleep up high in caves, barns, trees, and even people's attics! These bats (right) are sleeping hanging from a tree!

Raccoons are not choosy when making a home. While they like to nest up high in trees or barns, they also have been found nesting under houses and sheds, and even in abandoned cars!

Young raccoons high up in their tree-trunk home

Bats sleep upside down. **Tendons** that hold their feet closed keep them from losing their grip.

WOW! High-Voltage Nest

This stork's nest is on the top of a tower connecting power lines! In some countries, electric companies put special metal platforms on top of the towers for the storks to nest on. It's cheaper than having to repair the damaged towers!

11

Burrow Homes

Many types of animals live in burrows underground. Burrows can be a simple short tube to hide in or a big maze of tunnels and rooms. They provide shelter from predators and from the weather. Many **mammals** make burrows, but so do some insects, sea creatures, and even birds!

Meerkats live in burrow **dens** in the desert. They have several dens and move to a different one every day or two. The dens have many entrances so they can easily escape from danger.

12

Warthogs usually hide in other animals' old burrows. They back into the burrow so they can keep a lookout for danger. When they leave their burrow, they make a high-speed run for it in case any predators are waiting for them!

These Magellan penguins in Chile make their nests in burrows in the sandy soil. They live in big colonies, often several hundreds of thousands of them together.

WOW! Burrows – In Your Skin!

Scabies mites make their burrows in skin! This picture shows a mite burrowing a tunnel away from its entrance hole on the left.

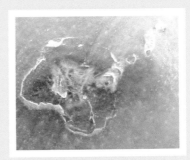

Homes to Go

Some animals can take their homes with them wherever they go. Their hard shells protect their bodies from **predators** and shelter them from the weather, too.

As a snail grows, its shell grows with it in a spiral shape. The growing shell is added at the open end of the old shell. Snails can hide inside their shells. They can also seal the entrance in dry weather to keep from drying up!

The shell the snail was born with ends up in the middle of the spiral.

American and Asian box turtles have a hinge on their lower shell. They can pull their legs and head in, and then close the shell using the hinge!

 # Little Armored Ones

"Armadillo" means "little armored one" in Spanish. This young three-banded armadillo can curl into a hard ball to stay safe from predators. Its tough, scaly skin is like armor. Armadillos also dig burrows with their strong legs and huge front claws. They eat ants and termites, using their long, sticky tongues.

Hermit crabs don't have shells of their own. So they make their home in any empty shell. When a crab grows too big for its shell, it will find a new one to move into.

More Master Builders

Some small animals can create the most amazing structures using teamwork, brains, and brute strength. Beavers can change a whole landscape. Little dung beetles work hard to make their own perfect home.

This beaver is building a dam. It has chopped down trees with its strong teeth and jaws. The dam has blocked the stream and turned this area into a large pond. In the pond is the beaver's domelike home, called a lodge. It can only be reached through underwater entrances!

 **WOW!** **Honduran White Bats' Tent Home**

These tiny white bats from Central America make their own tents from large leaves! They chew through the veins that support the leaf so it drops down to make a tent. They cling to the roof of the tent and get protection from rain and predators. The sun shining through the leaves makes the bats' white fur look green and helps hide them.

Dung beetles may be rollers, tunnelers, or dwellers. Rollers roll dung into balls and bury them to make their home. Tunnelers dig underneath piles of dung and then pull the dung into the tunnels. Dwellers simply live in piles of dung. Dung beetles lay their eggs in or near the dung, and they eat the dung, too!

These little dung beetles are stronger than they look. They can lift up to 50 times their own weight!

17

Spider Webs and Traps

Spiders weave the most amazing homes. They can make deadly webs to catch their food in, funnel-shaped holes to hide in, and even air chambers so they can breathe underwater!

A spider and its captured insect prey

Spiders produce silk from their **abdomen**. They make non-sticky silk for the spider to walk on, and sticky silk for trapping **prey**.

The mother nursery web spider will build a nursery "tent" when her eggs are about to hatch. The spider puts her egg sac inside and stands guard outside.

Building the nursery

This orange baboon tarantula is often called OBT for short. Some people call them Orange Bitey Things because they like to bite!

Many spiders, like this tarantula, make burrows to hide in. Funnel-web spiders make a burrow with a wide mouth-shaped entrance and then spin a large sheet of silk on top. Some of the silk threads extend beyond the burrow to act as trip wires. When an insect lands on the silk threads, the spider runs out of its burrow and pounces.

WOW! Scuba Diver Spider!

The diving bell spider, or water spider, lives its whole life under water, but it actually breathes air! It does this by building an underwater "diving bell" web that it fills with air. The spider lives almost entirely within the bell, darting out to catch prey animals that touch the bell or the silk threads that anchor it.

Water spiders eat, mate, and raise their young in their amazing webs.

19

Amazing Nests

Birds make lots of different types of homes. Common tree nests are works of art. Some birds make floating nests or dig burrows. Some birds make huge platforms. Others just scratch a small dent in the ground!

Penduline tit nest

Penduline tits make hanging pear-shaped nests using spider web, wool, animal hair, and soft plants as building materials (above). To fool predators, some nests have a false entrance above the real entrance, with a false room. The real nesting chamber has a hidden flap, sealed with sticky spider web!

Bank swallows are friendly birds. Hundreds of pairs of them are nesting close together on this sandbank. The nests, made of straw and feathers, are in rooms at the end of tunnels dug in the sand.

20

WOW! Boat-Building Bird

Grebes make floating nests on the surface of the water. Luckily, their young are able to swim from birth. Grebes are great swimmers. Their legs are too far back on their body to run well, and they often fall over!

Southern masked weavers make really complicated nests, woven from reeds, palm leaves, or grass. Males weave about 25 nests each season. When a female arrives, the male displays his nests. Females like new, green nests. If they have faded to brown, the female won't know how old they are. Males often destroy their old nests to put fresh ones in their place. The female will line her chosen nest with soft grass and feathers.

Starting a nest

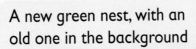

A new green nest, with an old one in the background

21

Glossary

abdomen (AB-duh-mun)
The back segment of the body
of an insect.

burrows (BUR-ohz)
Holes in the ground made by
animals for shelter or protection.

colonies (KAH-luh-neez)
Groups of animals in a particular
place that belong to one species.

dens (DENZ)
Shelters or resting places of
wild animals.

dung (DUNG)
Waste matter of an animal.

formic acid (FOR-mik A-sid)
A colorless, strong-smelling acid
that irritates the skin.

gland (GLAND)
A cell or group of cells that
makes and secretes a substance
such as wax.

hexagonal (hek-SAH-guh-nul)
Having six angles and six sides.

larvae (singular *larva*)
(LAHR-vee)
The young wormlike stage of
many insects after they hatch
from the egg.

mammals (MA-mulz)
Animals that feed their young
with milk, have a backbone, and
have skin covered with hair.

predators (PREH-duh-terz)
Animals that live by killing
and eating other animals.

structures (STRUK-churz)
Things that have been built.

prey (PRAY)
An animal hunted or killed
by another animal for food.

tendons (TEN-dinz)
Tough cords that link muscle
to bone.

Websites

For web resources related to the
subject of this book, go to:
www.windmillbooks.com/weblinks
and select this book's title.

23

Read More

George, Lynn. *Termites: Mound Builders*. Animal Architects. New York: PowerKids Press, 2011.

Kelly, Irene. *Even an Ostrich Needs a Nest: Where Birds Begin*. New York: Holiday House, 2009.

Simon, Seymour. *Spiders*. New York: HarperCollins, 2007.

Index

A
albatross 4
ants 7, 9
armadillo 15

B
bats 5, 10, 11, 17
beavers 16
bees 8
burrows 5, 12, 13, 20

C
colonies 6, 7
crabs 5, 15

D
dung beetles 17

F
fiddler crabs 5
funnel web spiders 19

G
grebes 21

H
hermit crab 15

L
larvae 8, 9
lodges 16

M
meerkat 12
mites 13
monitor lizards 7
mounds 6, 7

N
nests 4, 7, 8, 9, 11, 20, 21
nursery web spider 18

P
penduline tits 20
penguins 13

R
raccoon 10

S
shells 14, 15
snails 14
spiders 18, 19
stork 11

T
tarantula 19
termites 6
trees 10, 16
turtles 14

W
warthogs 13
wasps 8, 9
water spider 19
weaver ants 9
weaver birds 21
webs 18, 19
wood ants 7